Parenting

Raising Faithful Grade- Schoolers

Augsburg Fortress, Minneapolis

Contents

INTERSECTIONS
Small Group Series

Parenting
Raising Faithful Grade-Schoolers

Developed in cooperation with the Division for Congregational Ministries

George S. Johnson, series introduction
John Roberto, Center for Ministry Development editor
John Trokan and Nancy Trokan, contributors
Heather Hooper, Laurie J. Hanson, Elizabeth Drotning, and Jill Carroll Lafferty, editors
The Wells Group, series design
Cover: © 2001 PhotoDisc

Materials identified as *LBW* are from *Lutheran Book of Worship*, copyright 1978.

Scripture quotations are from New Revised Standard Version Bible, copyright 1989 Division of Christian Education of the National Council of the Churches of Christ in the United States of America. Used by permission.

Introduction

A quick look at the family section of your local bookstore will reveal dozens of books about parenting. What you probably will not find among these titles is a book about parenting and faith growth. *Parenting: Raising Faithful Grade-Schoolers* is specifically designed for parents of grade-school children. It provides an understanding of the unique characteristics of older (grade-school) children and ideas and strategies for nurturing faith in their lives by sharing Christian values, celebrating rituals, praying together, serving those in need, and developing a strong family life. *Parenting: Raising Faithful Grade-Schoolers* also suggests ways that you can continue growing as you walk with your child in faith.

Parenting: Raising Faithful Grade-Schoolers will help you develop skills for nurturing the Christian faith by:

- praying with your children
- reflecting on faith in daily life
- communicating effectively
- giving unconditional love
- telling the biblical story
- sharing your faith in Jesus Christ
- celebrating the Christian faith through rituals and traditions
- performing acts of service for those in need

The grade-school years present the family with a whole new series of challenges. Children's physical, intellectual, emotional, and social growth means that they are engaged in building and creating their own personalities. Their world is now broadened to include school and community activities as well as new friends. This is also an exciting time for faith growth.

Children are becoming capable of hearing their parents' expression of faith and their church's expression of faith. They are becoming capable of understanding the stories of Jesus and the church. They are realizing that they are members of our faith community. These new capacities and interests make for an exciting time of growth in the life of the family.

Our hope is to promote opportunities for families with older children to continue growing in faith. We hope you find the insights and ideas a source of support and encouragement in your task of parenting for faith growth.

Developmental assets

Search Institute, a research and educational organizaton in Minneapolis, has compiled a list of 40 developmental assets for elementary-aged children. (See page 52.) These assets are components identified in the lives of healthy, happy, well-adjusted children. They are named in this course as an awareness-raising guide as we work to raise healthy, faithful children.

Baptismal promises

This baptismal symbol appears in each chapter next to activities that remind us of the promises we make when our children are baptized.

SMALL GROUP SERIES

Welcome into the family of those who are part of small groups! Intersections Small Group Series will help you and other members of your group build relationships and discover ways to connect the Christian faith with your everyday life.

This book is prepared for those who want to make a difference in this world, who want to grow in their Christian faith, as well as for those who are beginning to explore the Christian faith. The information in this introduction to the Intersections small group experience can help your group make the most out of your time together.

Biblical encouragement

Do not be conformed to this world, but be transformed by the renewing of your minds, so that you may discern what is the will of God—what is good and acceptable and perfect. Romans 12:2.

Small groups provide an atmosphere where the Holy Spirit can transform lives. As you share your life stories and learn together, God's Spirit can work to enlighten and direct you.

Strength is provided to face the pressures to conform to forces and influences that are opposed to what is "good and acceptable and perfect." To "be transformed" is an ongoing experience of God's grace as we take up the cross and follow Jesus. Changed lives happen as we live in community with one another. Small groups encourage such change and growth.

What is a small group?

A number of definitions and descriptions of the small group ministry experience exist throughout the church. Roberta Hestenes, a Presbyterian pastor and author, defines a small group as an intentional face-to-face gathering of three to twelve people who meet regularly with the common purpose of discovering and growing in the possibilities of the abundant life.

Whatever definition you use, the following characteristics are important.

Small—Seven to ten people is ideal so that everyone can be heard and no one's voice is lost. More than twelve members makes genuine caring difficult.

Intentional—Commitment to the group is a high priority.

Personal—Sharing experiences and insights is more important than mastering content.

Conversational—Leaders that facilitate conversation, rather than teach, are the key to encouraging participation.

Friendly—Having a warm, accepting, nonjudgmental atmosphere is essential.

Christ-centered—The small-group experience is biblically based, related to the real world, and founded on Christ.

Features of Intersections Small Group Series

A small-group model

A number of small-group ministry models exist. Most models include three types of small groups:

- *Discipleship groups*—where people gather to grow in Christian faith and life;

- *Support and recovery groups*—which focus on special interests, concerns, or needs; and

- *Ministry groups*—which have a task-oriented focus.

Intersections Small Group Series offers material for all of these.

For discipleship groups, this series offers a variety of courses with Bible study at the center. What makes a discipleship group different from traditional group Bible studies? In discipleship groups, members bring their life experience to the exploration of the biblical material.

For support and recovery groups, Intersections Small Group Series offers topical material to assist group members in dealing with issues related to their common experience, hurt, or interest. An extra section of facilitator helps in the back of the book will assist leaders of support and recovery groups to anticipate and prepare for special circumstances and needs that may arise as group members explore a topic.

Ministry groups can benefit from an environment that includes prayer, biblical reflection, and relationship building, in addition to their task focus.

Four essentials

Prayer, personal sharing, biblical reflection, and a group ministry task are part of each time you gather. These are all important for Christian community to be experienced. Each of the six chapter themes in each book includes:

- Short prayers to open and close your time together.

- Carefully worded questions to make personal sharing safe, nonthreatening, and voluntary.

- A biblical base from which to understand and discover the power and grace of God. God's Word is the compass that keeps the group on course.

- A group ministry task to encourage both individuals and the group as a whole to find ways to put faith into action.

Flexibility

Each book contains six chapter themes that may be covered in six sessions or easily extended for groups that meet for a longer period of time. Each chapter theme is organized around two to three main topics with supplemental material to make it easily adaptable to your small group's needs. You need not use all the material. Most themes will work well for 1½- to 2-hour sessions, but a variety of scheduling options is possible.

Bible-based

Each of the six chapter themes in the book includes one or more Bible texts printed in its entirety from the New Revised Standard Version of the Bible. This makes it easy for all group members to read and learn from the same text. Participants will be encouraged through questions, with exercises, and by other group members to address biblical texts in the context of their own lives.

User-friendly

The material is prepared in such a way that it is easy to follow, practical, and does not require a professional to lead it. Designating one to be the facilitator to guide the group is important, but there is no requirement for this person to be theologically trained or an expert in the course topic. Many times options are given so that no one will feel forced into any set way of responding.

Group goals and process

1. Creating a group covenant or contract for your time together will be important. During your first meeting, discuss these important characteristics of all small groups and decide how your group will handle them.

Confidentiality—Agreeing that sensitive issues that are shared remain in the group.

Regular attendance—Agreeing to make meetings a top priority.

Nonjudgmental behavior—Agreeing to confess one's own shortcomings, if appropriate, not those of others, and not giving advice unless asked for it.

Prayer and support—Being sensitive to one another, listening, becoming a caring community.

Accountability—Being responsible to each other and open to change.

Items in your covenant should be agreed upon by all members. Add to the group covenant as you go along. Space to record key aspects is included in the back of this book. See page 51.

2. Everyone is responsible for the success of the group, but do arrange to have one facilitator who can guide the group process each time you meet.

The facilitator is not a teacher or healer. Teaching, learning, and healing happen from the group experience. The facilitator is more of a shepherd who leads the flock to where they can feed and drink and feel safe.

Remember, an important goal is to experience genuine love and community in a Christ-centered atmosphere. To help make this happen, the facilitator encourages active listening and honest sharing. This person allows the material to facilitate opportunities for self-awareness and interaction with others.

Leadership is shared in a healthy group, but the facilitator is the one designated to set the pace, keep the group focused, and enable the members to support and care for each other.

People need to sense trust and freedom as the group develops; therefore, avoid "shoulds" or "musts" in your group.

3. Taking on a group ministry task can help members of your group balance personal growth with service to others.

In your first session, identify ways your group can offer help to others within the congregation or in your surrounding community. Take time at each meeting to do or arrange for that ministry task. Many times it is in the doing that we discover what we believe or how God is working in our lives.

4. Starting or continuing a personal action plan offers a way to address personal needs that you become aware of in your small-group experience.

For example, you might want to spend more time in conversation with a friend or spouse. Your action plan might state, "I plan to visit with Terry two times before our next small-group meeting."

If you decide to pursue a personal action plan, consider sharing it with your small group. Your group can be helpful in at least three ways: by giving support; helping to define the plan in realistic, measurable ways; and offering a source to whom you can be accountable.

5. Prayer is part of small-group fellowship. There is great power in group prayer, but not everyone feels free to offer spontaneous prayer. That's okay.

Learning to pray aloud takes time and practice. If you feel uncomfortable, start with simple and short prayers. And remember to pray for other members between sessions.

Use page 51 in the back of this book to note prayer requests made by group members.

6. Consider using a journal to help reflect on your experiences and insights between meeting times.

Writing about feelings, ideas, and questions can be one way to express yourself; plus it helps you remember what so often gets lost with time.

The "Daily Walk" component includes material that can get your journaling started. This, of course, is up to you and need not be done on any regular schedule. Even doing it once a week can be time well spent.

How to use this book

The material provided for each session is organized around some key components. If you are the facilitator for your small group, be sure to read this section carefully.

The facilitator's role is to establish a hospitable atmosphere and set a tone that encourages participants to share, reflect, and listen to each other. Some important practical things can help make this happen.

- Whenever possible meet in homes. Be sure to provide clear directions about how to get there.

- Use name tags for several sessions.

- Place the chairs in a circle and close enough for everyone to hear and feel connected.

- Be sure everyone has access to a book; preparation will pay off.

- Have Bibles available and encourage participants to bring their own.

Welcoming

In this study, parents and guardians of young children can come together to explore how to nurture faith in their family and the lives of their children. This study provides a balance between understanding the faith of older children and developing practical ideas and strategies to nurture faith at home. Encourage the participants to practice the ideas they explore at home during the week. Parents and guardians of older children need encouragement and support in their efforts to build a family of faith!

Make necessary arrangements so that the physical and emotional environment for this group is as relaxed and comfortable as possible. Encourage people to come as they are, whether in business suits or gardening clothes. Make arrangements for child-care options to be available. Seek volunteer caregivers or shared child-care opportunities so that financial constraints do not keep people from attending.

Create a cozy atmosphere. Comfortable seating and space where everyone can converse with one another and be part of the group is vital. Encourage people to bring photos of their children to share with the group.

Focus

Each of the six chapter themes in this book has a brief focus statement. Read it aloud. It will give everyone a sense of the direction for each session and provide some boundaries so that people will not feel lost or frustrated trying to cover everything. The focus also connects the theme to the course topic.

Community building

This opening activity is crucial to a relaxed, friendly atmosphere. It will prepare the ground for gradual group development. Two "Community Building" options are provided under each theme. With the facilitator giving his or her response to the questions first, others are free to follow.

One purpose for this section is to allow everyone to participate as he or she responds to nonthreatening questions. The activity serves as a check-in time when participants are invited to share how things are going or what is new.

Make this time light and fun; remember, humor is a welcome gift. Use fifteen to twenty minutes for this activity in your first few sessions and keep the entire group together.

During your first meeting, encourage group members to write down names and phone numbers (when appropriate) of the other members, so people can keep in touch. Use page 50 for this purpose.

Discovery

This component focuses on exploring the theme for your time together, using material that is read and questions and exercises that encourage sharing of personal insights and experiences.

Reading material includes a Bible text with supplemental passages and commentary written by the topic writer. Have volunteers read the Bible texts aloud. The main passage to be used is printed so that everyone operates from a common translation and sees the text.

"A Further Look" is included in some places to give you additional study material if time permits. Use it to explore related passages and questions. Be sure to have extra Bibles handy.

Questions and exercises related to the theme will invite personal sharing and storytelling. Keep in mind that as you listen to each other's stories, you are inspired to live more fully in the grace and will of God. Such exchanges make Christianity relevant and transformation more likely to happen. Caring relationships are key to clarifying one's beliefs. Sharing personal experiences and insights is what makes the small group spiritually satisfying.

Most people are open to sharing their life stories, especially if they're given permission to do so and they know someone will actively listen. Starting with the facilitator's response usually works best. On some occasions you may want to break the group into units of three or four persons to explore certain questions. When you reconvene, relate your experience to the whole group. Appoint someone to start the discussion.

Wrap-up

Plan your schedule so that there will be enough time for wrapping up. This time can include work on your group ministry task, review of key discoveries during your time together, identifying personal and prayer concerns, closing prayers, and the Lord's Prayer.

The facilitator can help the group identify and plan its ministry task. Introduce the idea and decide on your group ministry task in the first session. Tasks need not be grandiose. Activities might include:

- Ministry in your community, such as adopting a food shelf, clothes closet, or homeless shelter; sponsoring equipment, food, or clothing drives; or sending members to staff the shelter.

- Ministry to members of the congregation, such as writing notes to those who are ill or bereaved.

- Congregational tasks where volunteers are always needed, such as serving refreshments during the fellowship time after worship, stuffing envelopes for a church mailing, or taking responsibility for altar preparations for one month.

Depending upon the task, you can use part of each meeting time to carry out or plan the task.

In the "Wrap-up," allow time for people to share insights and encouragement and to voice special prayer requests. Just to mention someone who needs prayer is a form of prayer. The "Wrap-up" time may include a brief worship experience with candles, prayers, and singing. You might form a circle and hold hands. Silence can be effective. If you use the Lord's Prayer in your group, select the version that is known in your setting. There is space on page 50 to record the version your group uses. Another closing prayer is also printed on page 50. Before you go, ask members to pray for one another during the week. Remember also any special concerns or prayer requests.

Daily walk

Seven Bible readings and a verse, thought, and prayer for the journey related to the material just discussed are provided for those who want to keep the theme before them between sessions. These brief readings may be used for devotional time. Some group members may want to memorize selected passages. The Bible readings also can be used for supplemental study by the group if needed. Prayer for other group members also can be part of this time of personal reflection.

A word of encouragement

No material is ever complete or perfect for every situation or group. Creativity and imagination will be important gifts for the facilitator to bring to each theme. Keep in mind that it is in community that we are challenged to grow in Jesus Christ. Together we become what we could not become alone. It is God's plan that it be so.

For additional resources and ideas see *Starting Small Groups—and Keeping Them Going* (Minneapolis: Augsburg Fortress, 1995).

1 Nurturing the Faith of Grade-Schoolers

Focus

The grade-school years are exciting times for family life. Children are developing physically, intellectually, emotionally and spiritually—presenting parents with new challenges and opportunities for nurturing faith growth.

Community building

Option

Share responses to the four unfinished sentences with each other.

- **One of the best things about being a parent of a grade-school child is...**

- **One of the most challenging things about being a parent of a grade-school child is...**

- **One thing I've learned from my child is...**

- **One thing I still need to learn as a parent of a grade- school child is...**

Introduce yourselves to one another. Share your children's names and their ages. Reminisce about the year you were eight years old. Have everyone share the first and second questions, then have each person answer a different question from the list.

a. Where were you living?
b. What was your home like?
c. What was your bedroom like?
d. What was your favorite hiding place?
e. What was your favorite TV/radio program?
f. At mealtimes, where did you sit?
g. What was conversation like in the family?
h. Was there a "warm" person for you in the family?
i. Were there "happy times" in your family life?
j. Did your family praise you? For what?
k. Did you look up to anyone in your family?
l. If so, what was so special about this person?
m. How did your family deal with problems?
n. If you could change one thing about your family of origin, what would it be?
o. In what way has your childhood affected the person you are today?

Now think about your grade-school child.

- What are some of the changes you are noticing in your child at this age?

- As a group, describe the important characteristics of the grade-school child.

Opening prayer

Loving God, we give you thanks for our children—for their faith and joy, their energy and spirit. Open our eyes to the marvelous potential in them and help us to see you at work in their lives each day. Amen

Discovery

The growth of the grade-school child

Grade-school children are developing physically, intellectually, emotionally and spiritually. Much of a parent's energy in these years is spent on the routine activities of providing for these needs. For many parents, little energy is left over for the emotional, intellectual and spiritual needs of other family members.

Thinking in new ways

During the grade-school years, children learn to think in new ways. They are better able to connect their personal learning and experiences with similar events in family life and in the world. Children are capable of hearing their parents' expression of faith, capable of joining in prayerful celebrations of that faith and capable of the initial integration of religious stories into their lives. As their intellectual capacities grow, our children need us to:

  a. teach them life skills of communication and survival
  b. provide opportunities for and show interest in further intellectual development
  c. allow them to fail and accept their mistakes
  d. encourage and affirm self-reliance
  e. express our faith, make them a part of our living, breathing faith and invite them to a more active participation in our larger faith community

The child becomes capable of capturing life and meanings in narrative and stories. The child can sort out the real from the make-believe, the actual from fantasy. Children are becoming capable of understanding the stories of Jesus and the church. This is why it is important for parents to share family faith stories as well as biblical and church stories with children.

A further look

Relating in new ways

Christian parents need to set firm limits while keeping channels of communication open and clear and be ready for questions and trials. The child's social development can be the most challenging for parents. Careful listening and encouragement are needed from parents to enable children to realize that they are not alone as they face this new world of social growth.

Discovery

Building a personality

Our children's physical, intellectual and social growth means that they are engaged in building and creating their own personalities. Important tasks to be accomplished during these years are the development of confidence and a sense of competence. This sense of competence grows in families which show unconditional love for each other.

- Which insights about grade-school children affirmed your own experience?
- What new insights about grade-school children did you discover?
- How does understanding the characteristics of older children help you become a more effective parent?

The faith of older children

Discuss the questions.

- What are you noticing about the faith of your child at this age? What's important to them, what questions are they asking, what interests them?
- Why do you want to pass on the Christian faith to your child(ren)?

Psalm 78:5-7

Together read the
Scripture passage aloud.

**5 He established a decree in Jacob,
and appointed a law in Israel,
which he commanded our ancestors
to teach to their children;
6 that the next generation might know them,
the children yet unborn,
and rise up and tell them to their children,
7 so that they should set their hope in God,
and not forget the works of God,
but keep his commandments;**

Read and reflect on
these thoughts about
nurturing the faith of
older children. Then
discuss the closing
questions.

Children normally enter a second stage of faith growth at about age six and remain there until about eleven or twelve. It is during this period that the children become aware of the many, often confusing, interpretations of faith, such as the traditions of Hanukkah and Christmas. As a child's experience broadens, so does his or her faith.

Older children's faith is marked by a more ordered approach, which begins to distinguish past, present and future. With this approach, life becomes a kind of story—the story of my being, my family, is intimately connected to my God. This is critically important for us to understand as parents. The most effective way for us to pass on faith to grade-school children is through stories of our faith:

> a. stories of loss and failure
> b. biblical stories of Moses, David, Abraham and the prophets
> c. stories of who your child's heroes and heroines are
> d. stories of those who have given meaning to our lives
> e. stories of modern-day "saints" of all cultures
> f. stories of civic leaders who make a difference in social justice
> g. stories of the faith of our own ancestors

It is through the shared story that we nurture a vision of meaning within our children that will help them to construct a broader view of the world with broader loyalties to God.

- Which insights about the faith of grade-schoolers affirmed your own experience?

- What new insights about the faith of grade-school children did you discover? How can these insights help you share the Christian faith with your child?

13

Consider this

PhotoDisc Inc. © 2001

Search Institute has identified a framework of 40 developmental assets for elementary-age children 6-11 years old. These 40 assets help children start out right and grow up healthy, well- adjusted, and strong. The 40 assets are grouped into eight categories: Support, Empowerment, Boundaries and Expectations, Constructive Use of Time, Commitment to Learning, Positive Values, Social Competencies, Positive Identity.

Throughout this book, we will connect children's spiritual growth with their overall growth using the Search assets.

To explore the importance of the assets for family life, review the following assets: 1, 2, 7, 8, 14, 16, 19, 24, 25, 38, and 39. (See pages 52 and 53 for a list of the assets.) Then discuss the following questions.

■ **How important are these assets for nurturing the faith growth of young children?**

■ **How can you strengthen your practice of these assets?**

Group goals and ministry task

Refer to pages 6–7 in this book. Read about group goals and group ministry tasks. Form groups of three to discuss group goals and a group ministry task. Talk about the following question and brainstorming topic. Then come back together as a group.

■ What do you hope to accomplish in this small-group course?

- Brainstorm group ministry task ideas that include the children of group members.
- Bring your ideas to the whole group for discussion and decision-making.

Experiencing ways to reach out in Christ's love is a powerful way to learn. Consider projects aimed at the needs of children, such as collecting food, toys, and clothing for parents and children in a local shelter, establishing a reading program for children at your local library or church, or providing tutoring or assistance to an elementary school or community center. Record your goals and group ministry task in the appendix on page 50.

Discovery

To learn more about parenting older children and to find a variety of family activities and ideas see page 54.

Psalm 139:1-4

1 O LORD, you have searched me and known me.
2 You know when I sit down and when I rise up; you discern my thoughts from far away.
3 You search out my path and my lying down, and are acquainted with all my ways.
4 Even before a word is on my tongue, O LORD, you know it completely.

An atmosphere of faith

The faith of children is most easily nurtured in an atmosphere of faith. How do we create an atmosphere of faith in our homes and families? Here are a few ideas:

Value our children's experiences. When we help children reflect on simple life experiences, we put them in touch with faith stories. Whether it's their first encounter with ocean waves, a conflict over sharing, or learning to tell the truth, we reinforce the belief that God is active in their lives.

Introduce the wisdom of the community. Keeping in mind children's simple life experiences, we share stories from the life of Jesus and the church that pertain to their faith story.

Create an atmosphere of dialogue. Here we attempt to relate the story of our children with the story of our faith. We want them to see that the God of our faith, who has been at work throughout history, is at work in their lives and in their story.

Gently challenge toward response. We ask a few questions and make a few suggestions to help our children live their faith. We cannot force a response, but try to encourage and support genuine responses to God.

Reflect on the questions individually and then discuss responses with the group.

■ How do you try to create an atmosphere of faith at home with your grade-schooler?

■ How would you use the four suggestions in your family? Think of practical ways you can use these ideas.

A further look

Read the passage and then take time, individually, to write your own responses. Share your insights with the group.

A parent's baptismal promise

At baptism parents are asked to state what they want for their child. Parents promise to train their child in the practice of the Christian faith, to bring up their child to keep God's commandments as Christ taught us, by loving God and neighbor. What do you want for your child?

■ Take a few minutes now or during the week to consider what you want for your child(ren). State your intentions clearly. Stop and think about what you are committing to in the raising of your child. You might even put it in writing.

■ Think ahead to the day your child is on his or her own. How would you define success as a parent of your child? What role will faith play in his or her life?

Wrap-up

See page 9 in the intro-
duction for a description
of "Wrap-up."

Before you go, take time for the following:

- Group ministry task

- Review

See page 50 for sug-
gested closing prayers.
Page 51 can be used for
listing ongoing prayer
requests.

- Personal concerns and prayer concerns

- Closing prayers

Daily walk

Bible readings

Day 1
Matthew 13:1-9
and 18-23

Day 2
Matthew 13:31-33

Day 3
Matthew 13:44-46

Day 4
Matthew 21:18-22

Day 5
James 2:14-28

Day 6
Matthew 5:13-16

Day 7
Matthew 7:24-27

Verse for the journey

Keep alert, stand firm in your faith, be courageous, be strong.
Let all that you do be done in love. 1 Corinthians 16:13-34

Thought for the journey

Once upon a time, the story goes, a preacher ran through the
streets of the city shouting, "We must put God into our lives.
We must put God into our lives." And hearing him, an old
monk rose up in the city plaza to say, "No, sir, you are wrong.
You see, God is already in our lives. Our task is simply to recognize that."

Prayer for the journey

Dear Lord, help our family to know what is most important.
Help us to demonstrate our faith in you through all the things
we do together. Bless us as we work together at being a family
of faith, hope and love. Amen

2 Sharing Faith with Grade-Schoolers

Focus

Families share the Christian faith through words and actions, loving relationships and a caring environment.

Have Bibles on hand for every participant. Also have for review family faith sharing books, children's storybooks, and children's Bibles. See page 54 for suggestions.

Give the parents time to reflect on the Faith Journey activity and then invite each person to share one or two key moments.

Community building

Your faith journey

Using the faith journey timeline below as a guide, identify key moments in your faith journey—important dates, events, and people that have strongly affected your life. Use the following symbols on the line:

G = times when God was important to you
? = times of questioning or doubting your faith
+ = times when you grew spiritually
- = times when you went back spiritually
! = times when God's love was revealed to you

```
|------------|------------|------------|------------|------------|
0            10           20           30           40          today
```

Option

Complete the following unfinished sentences:

■ As a child, faith for me was...

■ As I grew, my understanding of faith changed. Now I see faith as...

■ If I could describe my faith in an image or symbol, it would be...

■ I want to nurture my child's Christian faith because...

Opening prayer

Listen, my people,
mark each word.
I begin with a story,
I speak of mysteries
welling up from ancient depths.
We must not hide
this story from our children
but tell the mighty works
and all the wonders of God.

Psalm 78:1-4 (adapted)

Encountering the Jesus story

The Gospels provide us with many insights into what the people of Jesus' time found fascinating about him. His followers were so fascinated with him, his message, and his actions that they dedicated their lives to him.

■ What did people find so fascinating about Jesus that they were willing to follow him?

■ What do you find fascinating about Jesus of Nazareth?

Jesus touched lives in so many ways:

Jesus totally embraced his humanity. He loved both the joy and the pain of life. Every time he breathed in, he was conscious that God had breathed out. At every moment everything came from the love of God. To catch a glimpse of Jesus experiencing the joy and pain of life, read the story of Jesus and Lazarus in John 11:1-45.

Discuss your responses to the question and then quietly read and reflect on these thoughts about encountering the Jesus story. You may want to read several of the Gospel stories. Discuss the questions.

Jesus came at life with energy and purpose; he was faithful to the mission entrusted to him by God. Jesus' faithfulness to God inspired his entire life, even his decision to sacrifice his life on the cross. (Review Jesus' mission in Luke 4:16-21 and Luke 7:18-23.)

Jesus demonstrated great care and compassion and called us to be as compassionate as God. Compassion is the experience of feeling another's life as one's own. Jesus feels and acts out of compassion when he sees the sick (Matthew 14:13-21), meets hungry people (Matthew 15:32-38 and Mark 8:1-9), hears a leper's petition, (Mark 1:40-42), and sees a widow walking in the funeral procession of her son (Luke 7:11-16).

Jesus' care and compassion moved him to heal and forgive. The desire to heal is found throughout the gospel portrait of Jesus. He seeks out the sick and possessed, and once word gets out, they begin to seek him out. Jesus' stories and teachings about forgiveness are matched by his actions. He forgives his disciples and those who crucified him. To explore Jesus' ministry of healing and forgiveness, read John 4:43-53, John 5:1-8, John 8:3-11, Luke 5:17-25, Luke 7:1-10, Luke 7:36-50, Luke 8:26-39, Luke 8:40-55, Luke 13:10-17, Mark 5:1-20, Mark 5:21-43, Matthew 8:28-34, Matthew 9:18-26, Matthew 20:29-34.

Jesus' love and compassion included everyone. Jesus had a special concern for those whom society said were worthless—the poor, outcasts (tax collectors and sinners), women and children, and the marginalized of society. Whoever society had dismissed, devalued, or forgotten, Jesus pursued. Jesus was not prejudiced; he took each person on his or her merits. The stories of the Samaritan Woman (John 4:1-42), Zacchaeus (Luke 19:1-10) and the Great Banquets (Luke 14:15-23 and Matthew 22:1-10) demonstrate how Jesus' love includes everyone.

Jesus came to serve, not to be served. He was a leader who exercised his power through service, and commanded his followers to do the same. "Whoever wishes to be great among you must be your servant, and whoever wishes to be first among you must be your slave; just as the Son of Man came not to be served but to serve, and to give his life a ransom for many" (Matthew 20:26-28).

Jesus is alive! He continues his ministry through the actions of the Holy Spirit. Those who believe in him experience a relationship with a living Jesus. "And remember, I am with you always, to the end of the age" (Matthew 28:20).

Discuss the questions.

■ What did you find fascinating about Jesus from these insights? How were you affirmed? What new perspectives on Jesus did you gain?

■ How can you help your children become fascinated by Jesus?

Discovery

Sharing the Jesus story with children

Discuss your responses to the questions. Quietly read and reflect on these thoughts about sharing faith with grade school children, then discuss the following questions.

■ Do you have any favorite gospel stories of Jesus (i.e., stories Jesus told or stories about Jesus)?

■ How and when would you like to share Jesus stories with your children?

Each of us comes to faith in Jesus through the people around us. One of the most important gifts we can give our children is to share with them our own faith journey. It is important to let our children know that we are still growing in our relationship with the Lord.

Of all the skills for sharing our faith with our children, telling the story of Jesus in ways children can understand is most essential. The Bible is the story of God's love for us; the very heart of our Christian faith. In it we learn God's expectations of us, both as individuals and as a community. Learning to understand this love and these expectations is a lifelong journey for each of us.

Jesus presents us with a unique view of how we ought to live our lives with God and each other. When people hear a gospel story, it holds different meanings for each one because each person will hear it on his or her own level. We need to let the Gospels speak to our lives at any age, for the full meaning of life is not learned suddenly but acquired gradually.

Children need to hear Bible stories at bedtime, mealtime, on holy days and holidays—in language they can easily understand. They can sing the Bible stories, dramatize the stories, and express them through the visual arts.

Review resources at this time: family faith sharing books, children's storybooks, and children's Bibles. See the resource list on page 54 for suggestions.

Sharing family faith stories is also vitally important. Telling our children about the lives of our parents and grandparents, their struggles and faith journeys, fosters a sense of connectedness and belonging to a family which transcends time.

■ Can you use the gospel stories identified in "Encountering the Jesus Story" section to nurture the faith of your children? If so, how?

■ What new opportunities can you find to share family stories of faith and Jesus stories with your children?

Consider this

Grade-school children are still quite dependent upon their parents for answers to their questions. During childhood, children ask many faith questions, such as:

Eyewire © 2001

a. Who is God?

b. Where is God?

c. Why did Jesus die? Where did he go on Easter Sunday?

d. What do we eat in heaven?

e. What if Grandma didn't go to heaven?

By responding with compassion and faithfulness you can open a door for sharing stories from your life and family, and from the Bible and the Christian tradition. Invite the child to grow and seek answers to his or her faith questions.

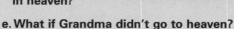

A further look

Read aloud the reflection on Baptism. Give the parents time to identify a symbol or image and then ask everyone to share with the group.

In Baptism we promise to guide our children in putting on the mind and heart of Christ. As Paul says, "Let the same mind be in you that was in Christ Jesus…"(Philippians 2:5). When we share the stories of Jesus and put their meaning into practice in our lives, we are putting on the mind and heart of Christ.

■ Think of a symbol or image for your family that reflects putting on the mind and heart of Christ.

■ Take time at home to create or find this symbol and display it in a special place to remind everyone of the importance of sharing and living the stories of Jesus.

Wrap-up

Before you go, take time for the following:

- Group ministry task

- Review

- Personal concerns and prayer concerns

- Closing prayers

Daily walk

Bible readings

Day 1
Luke 10:30-37

Day 2
Luke 15:11-32

Day 3
Luke 14:16-24

Day 4
Luke 16:19-31

Day 5
Luke 18:1-8 and 18:9-14

Day 6
Luke 12:16-21

Day 7
Luke 16:1-13

Verse for the journey

Your word is a lamp to my feet and a light to my path.
Psalm 119:105

Thought for the journey

When we adopt and live the values of Jesus we are putting on the mind and heart of Christ.

Prayer for the journey

O most merciful Redeemer, Friend and Brother;
May I know thee more clearly,
Love thee more dearly,
And follow thee more nearly. Amen.

Richard of Chichester, 1197-1253

3 Celebrating Rituals as a Family

Focus

Have a number of family ritual books available to review during the session. See the resource list on page 54 for suggestions.

Rituals are essential for our family life. Family rituals give us a sense of permanence, the assurance that even the most ordinary family activities are meaningful and significant.

Community building

Reflect on the questions and then invite people to share their stories with the group. Remember that this is a story-telling activity, not a group discussion.

In this chapter, we will have an opportunity to explore the importance of family rituals and create a family calendar of ritual celebrations to celebrate through the year with grade-school children.

- Does your family observe a religious ritual or celebration?

- If so, is this ritual meaningful to your family? Why or why not?

- If not, is there a religious ritual or celebration you would like to begin in your family?

Option

If possible, reflect and discuss one experience of worship or ritual celebration that really moved you.

- How were you moved? Why was this worship service or ritual celebration meaningful to you?

- Did you experience God through this worship service or ritual?

Opening prayer

1 Make a joyful noise to the LORD, all the earth.
2 Worship the LORD with gladness;
come into his presence with singing.
3 Know that the LORD is God.
It is he that made us, and we are his;
we are his people, and the sheep of his pasture.
4 Enter his gates with thanksgiving,
and his courts with praise.
Give thanks to him, bless his name.
5 For the LORD is good;
his steadfast love endures forever,
and his faithfulness to all generations.

Psalm 100

The importance of family ritual

Family rituals can be extremely simple or more involved. Some rituals occur daily—in the morning, before and after meals, or at bedtime—while others come along weekly, yearly, or once in a lifetime. They can be used to observe special days, such as Christmas and birthdays, as well as the more routine times in family life. Rituals are appropriate during times of celebration as well as loss.

When we observe rituals that have been handed down through the years or create new ones just for our families, we help our children to live and grow in faith. Rituals provide opportunities for children and parents to slow down and see God's presence in each day, think about the meaning of life's major events and daily happenings, and celebrate God's goodness.

- What role do rituals of faith play in your life today? In your family's life?
- What role would you like rituals of faith to play in your family's life?

Ecclesiastes 3:1-2, 4, 6-7

Read the Scripture passage together.

**1 For everything there is a season, and a time for every matter under heaven:
2 a time to be born, and a time to die;
a time to plant, and a time to pluck up what is planted;
4 a time to weep, and a time to laugh;
a time to mourn, and a time to dance;
6 a time to seek, and a time to lose;
a time to keep, and a time to throw away;
7 a time to tear, and a time to sew;
a time to keep silence, and a time to speak;**

Read about family and ritual.

Rituals of faith

Christianity is rich in rituals and traditions. Just as our church rituals define us as Christians, so too, our family rituals define the unity of our life together. Each family's rituals are a reflection of what they hold most sacred. Including simple prayers or Bible readings in our family rituals help connect the rhythms of our daily lives with God's active presence in our families.

Daily rituals

Read and discuss the question.

Rituals throughout the day help us to recognize and celebrate God's presence in our family life each day. Think about the many opportunities in your daily family life for celebrating a ritual of faith:

a. Prayer in the morning
b. Table blessings (before and after meals)
c. Telling and/or reading Bible stories
d. Leaving for school or work
e. Bedtime rituals: prayers, stories, blessings

■ What are the possibilities for daily rituals of faith in your family today?

Discovery

Seasons of the church year

Read about seasons of the church year and life transitions, and discuss the questions. Then engage the parents in developing a yearly ritual plan.

The possibilities for celebrating the seasons of the church year at home are numerous. For example, in one family's ritual for Ash Wednesday, each family member draws a symbol of a personal weakness that he or she intends to work on during Lent. This may range from vowing to make the bed each day, to putting on a happy face, to helping someone. These symbols are shared, placed in a foil-lined dish, and burned as an offering to the Lord. Afterward, the ashes are placed in a small jar on the dinner table where everyone can see them, as a gentle reminder of the Lenten promises.

Each season offers opportunities for celebrating rituals at home, for example:

Advent: daily Advent prayers, Advent wreath, Jesse tree, Advent calendars, Las Posadas

Christmas: blessing the Christmas tree, nativity scene, blessing for the Christmas meal, prayer while sharing Christmas gifts

Lent: Ash Wednesday prayer and simple meal, blessing a Lenten home cross, daily Lenten prayers, Holy Week seder meal, Holy Week Scripture readings

Easter: Easter eggs, decorating and praying with an Easter Christ candle

Be sure to consider the opportunities for celebrating ethnic holidays and feasts—even those from other ethnic groups.

- How do you currently celebrate the seasons of the church year in your family now?

- What are the possibilities for celebrating the seasons of the church year in your family today?

Life transitions and milestones

There are regular opportunities in family life for celebrating life transitions and milestones. Many people celebrate birthdays, anniversaries, first and last days of school, or a new job. Think about the possibilities in your family.

Discuss the questions below to see how rituals relate to your family life.

- Do you currently celebrate transitions and milestones in your family now?

- What are the possibilities for celebrating life transitions and milestones in your family today?

A further look

Complete the Yearly Rituals Plan, then share ideas with the group. Review the books and resources as you complete the plan.

Developing a yearly rituals plan

Think about the many opportunities for celebrating rituals of faith throughout the year: seasons of the Church, calendar seasons, and family transitions/milestones. Identify rituals that are already a part of your family life and new rituals that you would like to incorporate into your year. Use the chart on page 28 as a guide for planning your year. Add the dates for family milestones.

	Church season Calendar seasons Life transitions	Family Ritual Activity
December	Advent Christmas	
January	Epiphany Martin Luther King Jr.'s birthday	
February	Valentine's Day Ash Wednesday	
March	Lent	
April	Holy Week Easter	
May	Pentecost Mother's Day	
June	Father's Day	
July		
August	Start of school	
September		
October	Reformation Day	
November	All Saints Day	

Consider displaying your completed ritual plan on the refrigerator (or other prominent place in the house). Review your success at the end of the month or season and identify a ritual for the new month or season. Keep a record of your monthly rituals and action plans.

Consider this

The Search Institute has found that children can develop a positive identity when families have a sense of purpose and demonstrate a positive view of the future. Read the descriptions of assets 39 and 40 on page 53.

- ■ **How can these assets connect with your family's rituals?**

Begin a family scrapbook of rituals using drawings, snapshots, explanations, poems, reflections. Individual family members can add to the book by sharing their feelings about the event or simply recording the who, what, where, why, when of the event. This is a great way to pass on rituals to the next generation. It is also fun to see and read about your rituals as time turns them into memories.

A further look

Set up a prayer table with a large white candle, Bible, bowl of water, and small bowl of olive oil. Light the candle as you begin. Play instrumental music in the background.

Recalling the baptismal celebration

In this chapter, we will remember baptism through a prayer service.

- ■ Gather prayerfully around the table.

- ■ Have someone read about Jesus' baptism from Mark 1:9-11.

- ■ Pass the bowl of water around the group. One-by-one, dip your hand in the water and make the sign of the cross on your forehead. As each person does this, everyone prays: "May these waters renew the grace of your baptism in you."

- ■ Pass the bowl of olive oil around the group. One by one, dip your hand in the oil and make the sign of the cross on your forehead. As each does this, everyone prays: "May Christ strengthen you with his love and power."

- ■ Close this prayer service by reading Psalm 23.

Wrap-up

Before you go, take time for the following:

- Group ministry task

- Review

- Personal concerns and prayer concerns

- Closing prayers

Daily walk

Bible readings

Day 1
Luke 22:7-20

Day 2
Acts 2:37-41

Day 3
Psalm 95:1-7

Day 4
Acts 2:43-47

Day 5
Psalm 63:1-8

Day 6
Psalm 95:8-12

Day 7
Micah 6:6-8

Verse for the journey

O come, let us worship and bow down,
let us kneel before the Lord, our Maker!
Psalm 95:6

Thought for the journey

"To be effective and joyful parents, we must learn to celebrate all of family life, both the extraordinary—special days like birthdays, feast days and holidays—and the ordinary, finding God in our mealtimes, bedtimes, playtimes, and work times. We do this by creating ritual moments."

From *The Art of Tradition* by and © 1998 Mary Caswell Walsh.
Used by permission.

Prayer for the journey

Lord, guide us as we celebrate the seasons of faith in our family. Draw us closer together as we celebrate your presence throughout our day and throughout our year. Amen

4 Praying as a Family

Focus

Have prayer resources for families with grade-school children available to review. See the resource list on page 54 for suggestions.

Prayer is the very heart of our encounter and relationship with God. If prayer constitutes the soul of the Christian spiritual life, prayer must lie at the center of family spirituality.

Community building

Ask the parents to think about the role of prayer in their lives using the reflection questions.

Prayer in the family begins with parents. This chapter explores the role of prayer in your life and the life of your family. It offers a variety of approaches that you can utilize to strengthen the prayer life of families with grade-school children. We begin by taking time to reflect on the role of prayer in the life of your family today.

- Does your family pray? Is prayer part of your everyday life?
- If your family prays, what do they pray for or pray about?
- What could your family pray for or about?

Option

Describe your prayer life today using a color, a song or hymn, a weather condition, or a part of nature (sunset, mountains, ocean).

Read the prayer together.

Opening prayer

¹ It is good to give thanks to the LORD,
to sing praises to your name, O Most High;
² to declare your steadfast love in the morning,
and your faithfulness by night,
³ to the music of the lute and the harp,
to the melody of the lyre.
⁴ For you, O LORD, have made me glad by your work;
at the works of your hands I sing for joy.

Psalm 92:1-4

Romans 8:26-27

Read the Scripture
passage together.

[26] Likewise the Spirit helps us in our weakness; for we do not know how to pray as we ought, but that very Spirit intercedes with sighs too deep for words. [27] And God, who searches the heart, knows what is the mind of the Spirit, because the Spirit intercedes for the saints according to the will of God.

What is prayer?

Invite the group to share
their responses to the
questions and then read
the reflection on prayer.
Discuss the two follow-
ing questions.

■ How do you define prayer? Write a definition of prayer that reflects what you think about prayer at the present time.

■ What circumstances or events call you to prayer? When do you feel closest to God: alone? in a church setting? in a group? in nature?

From: *Prayer: Beginning Conversations
with God*, copyright © 1995 Augsburg
Fortress.

Richard Beckmen, author of *Prayer—Beginning Conversations with God* says this about prayer:

"Some people think prayer is 'saying a prayer'—speaking a particular intention to God. Prayer, however, can be understood more generally than that. Prayer, in a broad sense, links all aspects of our lives to God. God is present in all of life. We might set aside certain times and places for worship, but God is not absent from any time or any place. It is right and proper to pray at all times and in all places. (7-8)

"Prayer is centering our life in our relationship with God in Christ and allowing that center to be present in all we do. Christ will satisfy the hungering soul. Christ will bring solace to the pained heart. Christ will respond to the cry for mercy or the complaint for justice. Christ will be there when we simply need to feel that our relationship with God is warm and real. Christ will be there for rest, guidance, joy, love, and hope. In prayer we present our whole life and the lives of others to God, so that God may be known and lives may be touched by grace." (9)

■ Did you discover new insights about prayer in this essay? How do they affect that way you think about prayer?

■ How might you use these insights to strengthen your own prayer life?

Review the home
activity ideas.

Consider this

Family altar

Create a family altar for prayer and ritual. Find a place in your home (kitchen, family room) that you can set aside and decorate as your family altar or prayer space. Include the Bible, candles, art, photographs, prayer books, etc. on your altar.

Family prayer scrapbook

Begin a family book of prayers using drawings, snapshots, explanations, poems, reflections. This is a great way to pass on prayers to the next generation. It is also fun to see and read about them as time turns them into memories.

Prayer journals

Help your children create a prayer journal. Journal entries can include letters to God, prayers of the heart, art work, etc. Once a month invite the household to gather for prayer inviting members to share whatever they would like to share from their prayer journal.

Family prayer list

Consider keeping a family prayer list on wipe-off board and locating it where everyone in the family will see it. Encourage family members to write brief notes about problems or situations for which they would like the family to pray, as well as the names of people for which they would like the family to pray. Ask everyone to pray for the people and concerns listed there. Gather the family near the board daily or weekly for prayer.

Discovery

Prayer in the family

Discuss the question and then read the reflection on prayer in the family. Conclude by discussing the following question.

■ Should prayer be an important part of your family's life? Why or why not?

In family life, prayer can take many forms. Table and bedtime prayers may be the most common. There are opportunities throughout the day to acknowledge God's presence, such as being totally present for each other in times of pain, crisis or change. The first step in prayer is to open ourselves to God's presence.

By communicating clearly, we strengthen our family. By praying, we strengthen our relationship with God. Prayer is listening and talking, opening our hearts to the awareness of God's presence in our daily lives. We can teach our children the words of prayers (as Jesus taught us the Lord's Prayer) but our children can teach us much about communicating with God—about being open, honest and trusting. For children, prayer is a way of connecting their lives with God's life and God's will for them.

■ Have you prayed with your children? If so, how and when?

Forms of prayer

As you review six of the time-honored forms of prayer, reflect on how you practice each one in your life and the ways you can engage your children in this type of prayer.

Prayers of praise: We give praise to God for being good, for the mystery and majesty of God. Prayers of praise reflect our own attitude and ability to recognize others for their goodness.

Prayers of thanksgiving: We are grateful to God for the many gifts God shares with us. It can be a challenge to thank God for what we need even before we have it, trusting that God will provide for our needs in ways that are best.

Spontaneous prayers: Sometimes we are moved to pray on the spur of the moment. There are many ways spontaneously. One way is to use memorized prayers. Prayers that we hold in common and that are known to all help us to pray together as a community of faith.

Prayers of petition: One of the time-honored kinds of prayer is that of petition or asking God for what we and others need. Prayers of petition challenge us to recall our dependence on God.

Prayers of contrition: One of the well-established kinds of prayer is offering words of sorrow for our wrongdoing. In prayers of contrition we acknowledge that we are imperfect, that we make mistakes, that sometimes we choose wrong behavior that affects us and our relationship to God and others.

Reflecting on faith in daily life: Another form of prayer is reflection on our everyday life. It involves turning prayer time into a time of seeing and hearing God's presence in our daily lives and considering the significance and implications which this holds for us as disciples.

This would be a good time to display the prayer resources on page 54. Encourage parents to review the books as they consider how to incorporate prayer into their family life. Give examples of each of the forms of prayer.

Consider this

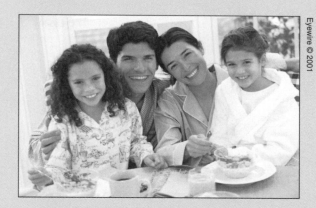

Eyewire © 2001

If time allows, the participants may want to practice the "Reflecting on Faith in Daily Life" prayer form as a group. Follow the process described here.

- ■ **With which of these six prayer forms are you most familiar and comfortable?**

- ■ **How can you use these six forms of prayer in your family?**

- ■ **Prayer takes practice. Identify times during the day or week that your family can more fully incorporate prayer into your family life, such as mealtime and bedtime.**

A further look

Baptism immerses us into a life with God who is Trinity: God is our parent and provider; Jesus is our redeemer and friend; the Holy Spirit is our sanctifier and consolation. The Lord's Prayer relates us to this life. This prayer reminds us who we are and what our Christian lives are all about. It is the foundational prayer of our faith.

- ■ What does the Lord's Prayer reveal to us about ourselves?
- ■ What does the Lord's Prayer reveal to us about prayer and the Christian life?

Wrap-up

Before you go, take time for the following:

- Group ministry task

- Review

- Personal concerns and prayer concerns

- Closing prayers

Daily walk

Bible readings

Day 1
Psalm 148

Day 2
Psalm 116

Day 3
Psalm 95:1-7

Day 4
Psalm 71

Day 5
Psalm 20

Day 6
Psalm 111

Day 7
Psalm 143

Verse for the journey

Ask, and it will be given you; search, and you will find; knock, and the door will be opened for you. For everyone who asks receives, and everyone who searches finds, and for everyone who knocks, the door will be opened. Matthew 7:7-8

Thought for the journey

"In the end, a life of prayer is a life with open hands where we are not ashamed of our weakness but realize that it is more perfect for us to be led by the Other than to try to hold everything in our own hands."

From *With Open Hands* by Henri J.M. Nouwen. Copyright © 1995 Ave Maria Press, P.O. Box 248, Notre Dame, IN 46556. Used with permission of the publisher.

Prayer for the journey

Lord,
   Make me an instrument of your peace.
   Where there is hatred, let me sow love;
   Where there is injury, pardon;
   Where there is doubt, faith;
   Where there is despair, hope;
   Where there is darkness, light;
   Where there is sadness, joy.

Francis of Assisi, 1182-1226

5 Serving as a Family

Focus

The call to serve and work for justice are central themes in the Bible. When families serve the needs of others, they follow in the footsteps of Jesus and grow in faith as a family.

Have children and family service books available to review. See the resource list for suggestions. It would also be helpful to have a list of church and community service projects for families with young children.

Community building

Reflect on what society says about the list. Use a phrase from a popular commercial or advertisement. Then comment on what Jesus says about these items.

   a. money...
   b. success...
   c. physical appearance...
   d. power...
   e. immediate gratification...
   f. possessions...
   g. equality...
   h. peace and forgiveness...
   i. pain and sorrow...
   j. poverty...

Option

Complete the following unfinished sentences.

■ **A social problem I wish we could fix is . . .**

■ **The world would be a better place if . . .**

■ **A person who embodies a life of justice and service is . . .**

■ **In the past, I was involved in serving others when . . .**

Read the prayer together.

Opening prayer

Lord, teach us what it means to be "poor in spirit" in a consumer society; to comfort those who suffer in our midst; to "show mercy" in an often unforgiving world; to "hunger and thirst for justice" in a nation still challenged by hunger and homelessness, poverty and prejudice; and to be "peacemakers" in an often violent and fearful world. Amen

Ask each person in the group to read aloud one Beatitude. Then discuss the meaning of each Beatitude.

Matthew 5:3-12

3 "Blessed are the poor in spirit, for theirs is the kingdom of heaven.
4 "Blessed are those who mourn, for they will be comforted.
5 "Blessed are the meek, for they will inherit the earth.
6 "Blessed are those who hunger and thirst for righteousness, for they will be filled.
7 "Blessed are the merciful, for they will receive mercy.
8 "Blessed are the pure in heart, for they will see God.
9 "Blessed are the peacemakers, for they will be called children of God.
10 "Blessed are those who are persecuted for righteousness' sake, for theirs is the kingdom of heaven.
11 "Blessed are you when people revile you and persecute you and utter all kinds of evil against you falsely on my account.
12 "Rejoice and be glad, for your reward is great in heaven, for in the same way they persecuted the prophets who were before you."

Living a Christian lifestyle

The Beatitudes invite us to take the risk of living as Jesus did. Just as in Jesus' day, the values contained in the Beatitudes run counter to the prevailing values of society.

- Review the community building activity. What would you add to your reflections on the wisdom of Jesus? How is Jesus' wisdom counter-cultural?

- Does your family embody the Beatitudes in daily life? Take a moment to review the Beatitudes and the contemporary reflections.

- Which of the Beatitudes are strengths in your family—ones you are working hard to live?

- Which of the Beatitudes need work in your family? Where do you need to grow as a family? How will you do this?

The call to justice and service

Our Christian faith calls us to work for justice; to serve those in need; to pursue peace; and to defend the life, dignity, and rights of all our sisters and brothers. This is the call of Jesus, the challenge of the prophets, and the living tradition of the church.

Isaiah 58:6-9

Read the Scripture passage together.

6 Is not this the fast that I choose:
to loose the bonds of injustice,
to undo the thongs of the yoke,
to let the oppressed go free,
and to break every yoke?
7 Is it not to share your bread with the hungry,
and bring the homeless poor into your house;
when you see the naked, to cover them,
and not to hide yourself from your own kin?
8 Then your light shall break forth like the dawn,
and your healing shall spring up quickly;
your vindicator shall go before you,
the glory of the LORD shall be your rear guard.
9 Then you shall call, and the LORD will answer;
you shall cry for help, and he will say, Here I am.

■ What does this passage from the prophet Isaiah say to you about the importance of justice and service in the Christian faith?

■ What are the implications of this passage for you and your family?

Engage the parents in exploring the scriptural foundation of the call to justice and service.
Form groups of two or three. Have each group read one Scripture passage and then answer the question.
Share brief reports with the entire group.

The Bible is rich in teachings on justice and service. Read your assigned Scripture passage and prepare a response to the following question.

■ What does this passage teach us about the importance of justice and service in the Christian faith?

    a. Leviticus 19:8-18
    b. Matthew 25:34-40
    c. Luke 4:16-19
    d. Luke 10:25-37
    e. Luke 16:19-31
    f. John 13:1-15
    g. 2 Corinthians 9:6-15
    h. James 2:1-17

■ Imagine what the world would be like if the principles embodied in the Bible became a reality in our time. What would it mean for your life, your family's life, your community, and our nation and world?

Living justice and service

Read this section quietly. Then discuss the questions.

Our families are the starting point and the center of a life of justice and service. As our family serves others, our children learn that faith is a verb, a way of acting Christ-like in the world. Faith is an active process deeply tied to how we live as a family, both for one another and in the world. Christ calls us to service, to "wash each other's feet" within our families and within our world. It is in answering this call to serve, to teach and heal, and to fight injustice, that we find community.

Consider adopting a service project each month or each season, especially during the Advent-Christmas and Lenten seasons. Some ways families can be involved in acts of service include:

a. preparing and serving a meal at a soup kitchen or homeless shelter
b. donating food for the local food bank; donating toys and clothes for children in need
c. visiting the elderly at a convalescent home or senior citizen facility
d. caring for the environment by recycling and by planting trees or a garden in your community
e. advocating for public policies that protect human life, promote human dignity, preserve God's creation, and build peace

■ How are individuals and families already involved in service in your church and community?

■ How is your church engaged in the work of justice and service?

■ What organizations in your community are engaged in the work of justice and service? Who do they serve?

■ How can your family become involved in justice and service—locally and globally?

Review assets 9, 26, and 27, and the benefits of service. Then discuss the questions.

Consider this

Three of the 40 assets for healthy development explicitly focus on the importance of the service: #9 (service to others), #26 (family values caring), and #27 (family values equality and social justice). Read about these on pages 52 and 53.

Involvement in service provides numerous benefits to children and parents alike:

Serving helps make the Christian faith real; it provides "hands-on" experiences and opportunities for growth.

Serving promotes healthy lifestyles and choices—it develops values and priorities that help children make positive choices.

Serving helps to develop positive self-esteem, self-confidence, and social skills. As people serve, they learn that they can make a difference in the world—that they have important things to contribute.

Serving teaches new skills and perspectives. Families see the world with a new perspective when they've been exposed to different people and different needs.

Serving nurtures a lifelong, commitment to service and justice involvement. Children who learn to serve when they are young are more likely to be service oriented when they are adults.

(Adapted from research by the Search Institute.)

■ **What do you see as the benefits of family service? Which benefits seem most important or significant to you?**

■ **How can involvement in service benefit you and your child?**

A further look

Baptism empowers us for our mission as Christians. Serving the needs of others and working for justice are essentials for all who are followers of Jesus.

It has been said that no one can do everything, but everyone can do something. Each of us has unique abilities, a certain amount of time, and financial resources. Each of us will someday give an account of our stewardship to God. Are there changes that you can make in allocating your talent, time, and treasure so that you can serve those in need and promote the work of justice—locally, nationally, globally?

Reaffirm your baptismal mission by making a family pledge for justice and service.

Wrap-up

Before you go, take time for the following:

- Group ministry task

- Review

- Personal concerns and prayer concerns

- Closing prayers

Daily walk

Bible readings

Day 1
Deuteronomy 30:15-20

Day 2
Isaiah 2:1-5

Day 3
Isaiah 61:1-2

Day 4
Psalm 146

Day 5
Luke 3:10-18

Day 6
Acts 4:32-35

Day 7
1 John 4:19-21

Verse for the journey

This is what God asks of you, and only this: That you act justly, love tenderly, and walk humbly with your God. Micah 6:8

Thought for the journey

The lessons we teach our children through our words and actions influence their commitment to justice and caring for the "least among us."

Prayer for the journey

God, true light and source of all light, may we recognize you in oppressed people and poor people, in homeless people and hungry people. May we be open to your Spirit that we may be a means of healing, strength and peace for all your people. Inspire us to use the varied gifts with which we have been blessed in the service of others. We ask this in the name of Jesus, your son and our brother! Amen

6 Relating as a Family

Focus

Have parenting and family enrichment books available to review during the session. See the resource list on page 54 for suggestions.

A strong home life is possible for every family. Developing your family's strengths, creating a family mission statement, and practicing the skills for effective family living are important ingredients in building a strong family.

Community building

Invite each person to share with the group his or her gift or strength and a story to illustrate it. Keep the focus on sharing and storytelling.

■ One of my greatest gifts or strengths as a parent of older children is…

■ Recall a story which illustrates one of your parenting gifts or strengths.

Option

Describe your family using a TV commercial, a TV show, Broadway musical or feature film, a popular song, or a popular book title.

Opening prayer

Gracious God, give us the strength and wisdom to build families on the foundations of love and compassion, kindness and generosity, humility and gentleness, forgiveness and peace. Amen

Building a strong family

Discuss the question and then ask one person to read the Scripture passage aloud. Conclude by discussing the following questions.

■ Take a moment to think about the qualities you want to see present in your family. What qualities do you want to describe your life as a family?

Colossians 3:12-17

12 As God's chosen ones, holy and beloved, clothe yourselves with compassion, kindness, humility, meekness, and patience. 13 Bear with one another and, if anyone has a complaint against another, forgive each other; just as the Lord has forgiven you, so you also must forgive. 14 Above all, clothe yourselves with love, which binds everything together in perfect harmony. 15 And let the peace of Christ rule in your hearts, to which indeed you were called in the one body. And be thankful. 16 Let the word of Christ dwell in you richly; teach and admonish one another in all wisdom; and with gratitude in your hearts sing psalms, hymns, and spiritual songs to God. 17 And whatever you do, in word or deed, do everything in the name of the Lord Jesus, giving thanks to God the Father through him.

The letter to the Colossians describes the essential qualities of a Christian family, as well as the Christian community.

■ How does this Scripture passage affirm your own hopes for your family life?

■ What would it be like if you lived this vision in your family?

Read the qualities and then discuss the questions.

Nick Stinnett and John DeFrain have interviewed thousands of families and identified qualities of strong families. Strong families are not problem-free, but rather have learned to harness their resources to surmount difficulties.

As you review the list of six strengths, which do you see present in your family now and which ones do you need to develop?

a. A strong family shares a sense of commitment and connectedness.

b. A strong family spends both quality and quantity time together sharing many areas of life.

c. A strong family engages in communication that is clear, open, frequent, and honest. Communication is the life-blood of a strong family.

d. A strong family appreciates one another and takes the time to let one another know this.

e. A strong family has a shared religious and moral core. For Christian families this center is the person of Jesus and the Gospel message of love and service.

f. A strong family is able to cope with crisis and times of stress in a positive manner.

■ Which strengths do you find present in your family today?

■ Which strengths do you want to develop in your family? How might you go about developing these strengths? What will need to change? What obstacles do you anticipate?

■ What is the role of the parent in building a strong family?

Form teams. Assign each team one category of assets. Have each team summarize briefly their assets and then suggest ways in which families with young children can put the assets into practice. Turn to pages 52 and 53 to review the assets. Discuss the questions.

Consider this

The 40 assets from Search Institute provide the building blocks that help children start out well and grow up healthy, well adjusted, and strong. Assets create a firm foundation for children from day one.

Many of the assets describe the qualities of a family that is actively promoting the growth of their children. Explore the implications of the assets for developing a family that promotes growth by reviewing the following assets:

a. Support: 1, 2, 6
b. Empowerment: 7-10
c. Boundaries and Expectations: 11, 14, 15, 16
d. Constructive Use of Time: 17-20
e. Commitment to Learning: 21-25
f. Positive Values: 26-31
g. Social Competencies: 32-36
h. Positive Identity: 37-40

Together with your team review the assets in your category and then suggest ways in which families with young children can put the assets into practice.

■ How important are these assets for nurturing positive growth in older children?

■ How can you strengthen the practice of these assets in your family?

A family mission statement

Share your responses to the question and then review the steps of writing a family mission statement.

■ How would you describe your family's mission today—in a phrase, image or symbol.

The creation of a family mission statement has been a significant event in the lives of many families. A family mission statement reflects the hearts and minds of the family members, and serves as a collective ideal of all the members of the family. A family mission statement involves making choices. For example, one family may choose to focus more energy on spending quality time together, while another family may seek to involve God more actively in most aspects of family life.

■ Take a moment to read Jesus' "mission statement" in Luke 4:16-19.

Adapted from *Smart Choices: Making Your Way Through Life* by Harold Eppley and Rochelle Melander, © 1998 Augsburg Fortress.

The first thing to remember when putting together your family mission statement is to keep it simple. If you make your family mission statement clear and concise it will be of more practical help to your family. Explore what is important to your family.

Second, remember that your family mission is unique to your family and connected to the overall mission of other Christians.

Third, as your family lives out the mission, know that it will affect not only the relationships within the family, but with others as well, including God. Consider how putting your family mission statement into practice will affect others in your lives.

Fourth, make sure that the goals agreed upon in your mission statement are within your family's power to accomplish. They should concentrate on actions important to your family rather than the responses of others.

Finally, your family mission statement can (and should) be evaluated and revised at any point in the future.

As you work today, consider your family's present situation.

■ What do you find most exciting about writing a family mission statement? Most challenging?

■ To write your mission statement, begin by choosing three key principles upon which you want to center your family life. Then choose three of the gifts with which God has blessed your family. In choosing these principles and gifts consider your family's current life circumstances and constraints. Ask your family: Which principles and gifts can best help us to carry out our mission at this time?

You did not write your family mission in stone, and for good reason. Mission statements are meant to be flexible. As we journey through life, God calls us to minister in various ways and situations. As our children grow, our roles and relationships are always changing. For this reason, we need to review and revise out family mission statements periodically.

Here are some questions you might want to ask your family when trying to decide if it is time to change your mission statement.

- Have our life circumstances changed since we wrote our family mission statement?

- Is our family mission statement making an ongoing positive difference in our lives?

- Is God calling us in a new direction in our lives?

Communicating effectively as a family

Begin by discussing the three questions. Then read the insights on effective community.

- The best way to communicate with children is…

- The hardest thing about communicating with my children is…

- The benefit of effectively communicating with my children is…

At the heart of effective communication is empathic listening—seeking first to understand, then to be understood. Once someone feels really listened to and understood he or she is more open to listening in return. The focus of effective communication is understanding others so you can speak in their terms rather than expecting them to understand your terms.

Here are several simple guidelines to remember when listening to your children:

a. Let go of your own experience as much as you can and enter the world of the other person.
b. Create a receptive atmosphere by listening attentively.
c. Try to be self-revealing to your children as you wish them to be with you.
d. Teach them to take responsibility for their own concerns and problems.
e. Use "I" messages as much as possible stating how you feel. For example, you can say, "I feel like my ideas aren't always heard," instead of saying, "You never do anything I want to do." These messages should not include blaming statements or commands, such as "I think you should act differently" or "You" statements, such as "You should be more..."

- What are the benefits of empathetic listening for your family?

- How can you use these insights to improve communication in your family? Think of an example when communication was difficult with your children. How can you improve that situation using these insights?

A further look

In Baptism we are given a new birth by water and the Holy Spirit. In the Letter to the Galatians, Paul challenges us to live in the Spirit. As Paul writes, "the fruit of the Spirit is love, joy, peace, patience, kindness, generosity, faithfulness, gentleness, and self-control" (Galatians 5:22-23).

- How has the Holy Spirit blessed your family with these fruits or qualities?

- Take a moment for prayer. Reflect on which of these fruits your family most needs now. Pray to the Holy Spirit to respond to your need.

Wrap-up

Before you go, take time for the following:

- Group ministry task

- Review

- Personal concerns and prayer concerns

- Closing prayers

Daily walk

Bible readings

Day 1
Romans 12:9-13

Day 2
John 15:12-17

Day 3
1 Corinthians 13:1-13

Day 4
Luke 6:37-39

Day 5
Philippians 2:1-11

Day 6
Ephesians 4:1-6

Day 7
Deuteronomy 6:1-9

Verse for the journey

Love is patient; love is kind; love is not envious or boastful or arrogant or rude. It does not insist on its own way; it is not irritable or resentful; it does not rejoice in wrongdoing, but rejoices in the truth. It bears all things, believes all things, hopes all things, endures all things. 1 Corinthians 13:4-7

Thought for the journey

The interaction between family members is the most important ingredient in effective family relationships.

Steven Covey. *The 7 Habits of Highly Effective Families 1998 Calendar.*
Provo, UT: Covey Leadership Center, 1997

Prayer for the journey

Lord, give our family the strength and courage to listen and communicate clearly, to forgive and comfort compassionately, and to love each other abundantly. Amen

Appendix

Group directory

Record information about group members here.

Names   **Addresses**   **Phone numbers**

_____

_____

_____

_____

_____

_____

_____

_____

_____

_____

_____

_____

Prayers

■ Closing Prayer

Lord God, you have called your servants
to ventures of which we cannot see the
ending, by paths as yet untrodden,
through perils unknown. Give us faith to
go out with good courage, not knowing
where we go, but only that your hand is
leading us and your love supporting us;
through Jesus Christ our Lord. Amen

From *Lutheran Book of Worship* (page 153) copyright © 1978.

(If you plan to pray the Lord's Prayer, record the
version your group uses in the next column.)

■ The Lord's Prayer

Group commitments

Do not be conformed to this world, but be transformed by the renewing of your minds, so that you may discern what is the will of God—what is good and acceptable and perfect. Romans 12:2.

■ For our time together, we have made the following commitments to each other

■ Goals for our study of this topic are

■ Our group ministry task is

■ My personal action plan is

Prayer requests

_____

_____

_____

_____

_____

_____

_____

_____

_____

_____

_____

_____

40 Developmental Assets for Elementary-Age Children

EXTERNAL ASSETS

ASSET TYPE	ASSET NAME	ASSET DEFINITION
Support	1. Family support	Family life provides high levels of love and support.
	2. Positive family communication	Parents and children communicate positively. Children are willing to seek advice and counsel from their parents.
	3. Other adult relationships	Children have support from adults other than their parents.
	4. Caring neighborhood	Children experience caring neighbors.
	5. Caring out-of-home climate	School and other activities provide caring, encouraging environments for children.
	6. Parent involvement in out-of-home situations	Parents are actively involved in helping children succeed in school and in other situations outside the home.
Empowerment	7. Community values children	Children feel that the family and community value and appreciate children.
	8. Children are given useful roles	Children are included in age-appropriate family tasks and decisions and are given useful roles at home and in the community.
	9. Service to others	Children serve others in the community with their family or in other settings.
	10. Safety	Children are safe at home, at school, and in the neighborhood.
Boundaries and Expectations	11. Family boundaries	The family has clear rules and consequences and monitors children's activities and whereabouts.
	12. Out-of-home boundaries	Schools and other out-of-home environments provide clear rules and consequences.
	13. Neighborhood boundaries	Neighbors take responsibility for monitoring children's behavior.
	14. Adult role models	Parents and other adults model positive, responsible behavior.
	15. Positive peer interaction and influence	Children interact with other children who model responsible behavior and have opportunities to play and interact in safe, well-supervised settings.
	16. Appropriate expectations for growth	Adults have realistic expectations for children's development at this age. Parents, caregivers, and other adults encourage children to achieve and develop their unique talents.
Constructive Use of Time	17. Creative activities	Children participate in music, art, drama, or other creative activities for at least three hours a week at home and elsewhere.
	18. Out-of-home activities	Children spend one hour or more each week in extracurricular school activities or structured community programs.
	19. Religious community	The family attends religious programs or services for at least one hour per week.
	20. Positive, supervised time at home	Children spend most evenings and weekends at home with their parents in predictable, enjoyable routines.

INTERNAL ASSETS

ASSET TYPE	ASSET NAME	ASSET DEFINITION
Commitment to Learning	21. Achievement expectation and motivation	Children are motivated to do well in school and other activities.
	22. Children are engaged in learning	Children are responsive, attentive, and actively engaged in learning.
	23. Stimulating activity and homework	Parents and teachers encourage children to explore and engage in stimulating activities. Children do homework when it's assigned.
	24. Enjoyment of learning and bonding to school	Children enjoy learning and care about their school.
	25. Reading for pleasure	Children and an adult read together for at least 30 minutes a day. Children also enjoy reading or looking at books or magazines on their own.
Positive Values	26. Caring	Children are encouraged to help other people.
	27. Equality and social justice	Children begin to show interest in making the community a better place.
	28. Integrity	Children begin to act on their convictions and stand up for their beliefs.
	29. Honesty	Children begin to value honesty and act accordingly.
	30. Responsibility	Children begin to accept and take personal responsibility for age-appropriate tasks.
	31. Healthy lifestyle and sexual attitudes	Children begin to value good health habits and learn healthy sexual attitudes and beliefs as well as respect for others.
Social Competencies	32. Planning and decision making	Children begin to learn how to plan ahead and make choices at appropriate developmental levels.
	33. Interpersonal skills	Children interact with adults and children and can make friends. Children express and articulate feelings in appropriate ways and empathize with others.
	34. Cultural competence	Children know about and are comfortable with people of different cultural, racial, and/or ethnic backgrounds.
	35. Resistance skills	Children start developing the ability to resist negative peer pressure and dangerous situations.
	36. Peaceful conflict resolution	Children try to resolve conflicts nonviolently.
Positive Identity	37. Personal power	Children begin to feel they have control over things that happen to them. They begin to manage frustrations and challenges in ways that have positive results for themselves and others.
	38. Self-esteem	Children report having high self-esteem.
	39. Sense of purpose	Children report that their lives have purpose and actively engage their skills.
	40. Positive view of personal future	Children are hopeful and positive about their personal future.

Chesto, Kathleen. *Family Prayer for Family Times—Traditions, Celebrations, and Rituals.* Mystic, CT: Twenty-third Publications, 1996.

———. *Raising Kids Who Care—About Themselves, About Their World, About Each Other.* Kansas City, MO: Sheed and Ward, 1996.

Coffey, Kathy. *Experiencing God with Your Children.* New York: Crossroad Publishing, 1998.

Cloyd, Betty Shannon. *Children and Prayer—A Shared Pilgrimage.* Nashville: Upper Rooms Books, 1997.

Dosick, Wayne. *Golden Rules—The Ten Ethical Values Parents Need to Teach Their Children.* San Francisco: HarperSanFrancisco, 1995.

Erickson, Kenneth A. *Helping Your Children Find Good About Themselves: A Guide to Building Self-Esteem.* Minneapolis: Augsburg Books, 1995.

Fitzpatrick, Jean Grasso. *Small Wonder—How to Answer Your Child's Impossible Questions About Life.* New York: Viking, 1994.

Fuchs-Kreimer, Rabbi Nancy. *Parenting as Spiritual Journey—Deepening Ordinary and Extraordinary Events into Sacred Occasions.* Woodstock, VT: Jewish Lights Publishing, 1996.

Halverson, Delia. *How Do Your Children Grow?—Introducing Children to God, Jesus, the Bible, Prayer, Church.* Nashville: Abingdon, 1993.

Hansen, Anne Marie Witchger, and Jim Vogt. *Kids Creating Circles of Peace.* St. Louis: Families Against Violence Advocacy Network/Institute for Peace and Justice, 2000.

Jones, Timothy. *Nurturing a Child's Soul.* Nashville: Word Publishing, 2000.

McGinnis, James and Kathleen. *Parenting for Peace and Justice.* Maryknoll, NY: Orbis Books, 1981.

McGinnis, James, Ken and Gretchen Lovingood, and Jim Vogt. *Families Creating a Circle of Peace.* St. Louis: Families Against Violence Advocacy Network/Institute for Peace and Justice, 1996.

McGrath, Tom. *Raising Faith-Filled Kids.* Chicago: Loyola Press, 2000.

Nappa, Mike and Amy. *52 Fun Family Devotions.* Minneapolis: Augsburg Books, 1994

Nelson, Gertrud Mueller. *To Dance with God—Family Ritual and Community Celebration.* New York: Paulist Press, 1986.

Nolte, Dorothy Law, and Rachel Harris. *Children Learn What They Live—Parenting to Inspire Values.* New York: Workman Publishing, 1998.

O'Neal, Debbie Trafton. *The Family Hand-Me-Down Book.* Minneapolis: Augsburg Books, 2000.

———. *Thank You for This Food.* Minneapolis: Augsburg Books, 1995.

Persky, Margaret McMillan. *Living in God's Time—A Parent's Guide to Nurturing Children throughout the Christian Year.* Nashville: Upper Room Books, 1999.

Reed, Bobbie. *501 Practical Ways to Teach Your Children Values.* St. Louis: Concordia Publishing House, 1998.

Wright, Wendy. *Sacred Dwelling—A Spirituality of Family Life.* New York: Crossroad, 1990.

Young, Peter. *Celebrate Life—Rituals for Home and Church.* Cleveland: United Church Press, 1999.

Zerheide, Jerry R. and Karen Johnson Zerheide. *In Their Own Way: Accepting Your Children for Who They Are.* Minneapolis: Augsburg Books, 2000.

For additional books for parents and recommended children's books go to cmdnet.org/parenting.nn

Name _____

Address _____

Daytime telephone _____

Please check the INTERSECTIONS book you are evaluating.

- ☐ The Bible and Life
- ☐ Caring and Community
- ☐ Death and Grief
- ☐ Faith
- ☐ Following Jesus
- ☐ Integrity
- ☐ Jesus: Divine and Human
- ☐ Managing Stress

- ☐ Parenting
- ☐ Parenting: Raising Faithful Preschoolers
- ☐ Parenting: Raising Faithful Grade-Schoolers
- ☐ Parenting: Raising Faithful Younger Adolescents
- ☐ Parenting: Raising Faithful Older Adolescents
- ☐ Peace
- ☐ Praying
- ☐ Reconcilable Differences
- ☐ Smart Choices

Please tell us about your small group.

1. Our group had an average attendance of _____.

2. Our group was made up of
   _____ Young adults (19-25 years).
   _____ Adults (most between 25-45 years).
   _____ Adults (most between 45-60 years).
   _____ Adults (most between 60-75 years).
   _____ Adults (most 75 and over).
   _____ Adults (wide mix of ages).
   _____ Men (number) and _____ women (number).

3. Our group (answer as many as apply)
   _____ came together for the sole purpose of studying this INTERSECTIONS book.
   _____ has decided to study another INTERSECTIONS book.
   _____ is an ongoing Sunday school group.
   _____ met at a time other than Sunday morning.
   _____ had only one facilitator for this study.

-------------------- FOLD CARD IN HERE, SEAL WITH TAPE, AND MAIL TODAY! --------------------

Please tell us about your experience with INTERSECTIONS.

4. What I like best about my INTERSECTIONS experience is

5. Three things I want to see the same in future INTERSECTIONS books are

6. Three things I might change in future INTERSECTIONS books are

7. Topics I would like developed for new INTERSECTIONS books are

8. Our group had _____ sessions for the six chapters of this book.

9. Other comments I have about INTERSECTIONS are

_____

Thank you for taking the time to fill out and return this questionnaire.

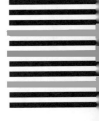

BUSINESS REPLY MAIL
FIRST-CLASS MAIL   PERMIT NO. 22120   MINNEAPOLIS, MN

POSTAGE WILL BE PAID BY ADDRESSEE

Augsburg Fortress
ATTN INTERSECTIONS TEAM
PO BOX 1209
MINNEAPOLIS MN 55440-8807